# INSIDE THE INDUSTRY
# ENTERTAINMENT

BY MARCIA AMIDON LUSTED

# INSIDE THE INDUSTRY
# ENTERTAINMENT

BY MARCIA AMIDON LUSTED

**ABDO**
Publishing Company

# CREDITS

Published by ABDO Publishing Company, 8000 West 78th Street, Edina, Minnesota 55439. Copyright © 2011 by Abdo Consulting Group, Inc. International copyrights reserved in all countries. No part of this book may be reproduced in any form without written permission from the publisher. The Essential Library™ is a trademark and logo of ABDO Publishing Company.

Printed in the United States of America,
North Mankato, Minnesota
112010
012011

 THIS BOOK CONTAINS AT LEAST 10% RECYCLED MATERIALS.

Editor: Mari Kesselring
Copy Editor: Erin Molta
Interior Design and Production: Christa Schneider
Cover Design: Christa Schneider

**Library of Congress Cataloging-in-Publication Data**
Lusted, Marcia Amidon.
  Entertainment / by Marcia Amidon Lusted.
      p. cm. -- (Inside the industry)
  Includes bibliographical references.
  ISBN 978-1-61714-799-9
  1. Performing arts--Vocational guidance--Juvenile literature. I. Title.
  PN1580.L87 2011
  791.023--dc22
                                2010041255

# TABLE OF CONTENTS

There are many opportunities to work in the entertainment industry, both in the spotlight and behind the scenes.

# IS AN ENTERTAINMENT JOB FOR YOU?

"Culture relates to objects and is a phenomenon of the world; entertainment relates to people and is a phenomenon of life."[1]

—*Hannah Arendt, German philosopher, 1906–1975*

You love to entertain. Maybe you play an instrument in a band, sing in a choir, or act in school plays. You love to watch movies, and you constantly listen to music on your iPod. As you start to think about your future, you wonder if your love of the arts and performing can translate into a career in the entertainment industry. What jobs might be available to you?

You know the most obvious ones: classical or popular musician, or an actor in a theater, on television, or in movies. You see big-name movie actors on magazine covers and on-screen, and you wonder what that kind of life is like. You notice rock stars on world tours or famous classical musicians performing in the biggest concert halls in the country and think that is extremely appealing. But you're not sure if you really have what it takes to succeed in this very competitive industry. What other entertainment jobs might be a possibility for you? You know a little about directors, usually from the special features section of a DVD, and you've seen conductors lead orchestras during concerts. How does someone land one of these jobs? What do these people do on a day-to-day basis?

## LOOKING TO THE FUTURE

The US Department of Labor publishes data of how many people are involved in the entertainment field and how it will change over the next decade. Overall, they project careers in the entertainment industry will grow by 10 to 15 percent.[2]

# ENTERTAINMENT: MORE THAN MEETS THE EYE OR EAR

When you think about entertainment careers, the first jobs that come to mind are the ones that involve performing in front of an audience. Both professional musicians and actors make their money from performances. Musicians perform live in theaters, churches, or concert halls. Actors perform in movies, on stage in theaters, or in television shows. Because these careers are the most visible and important to pop culture, they are usually the first career option someone interested in the entertainment arts considers.

However, these careers can be very competitive. Luckily, if you really want a career in entertainment, there are many options to consider. The music industry needs not only performers to play music, but conductors to organize orchestras and bands, to interpret music, and to run rehearsals. The music industry also needs composers to write new music and arrangers to adapt new or existing music for specific types of instruments or groups. Accomplished musicians are also needed to teach other musicians.

## A CREATIVE INDUSTRY

The entertainment business is essentially about creativity, which often means going in new directions from what the accepted forms are. As musician Charlie Parker puts it, "Music is your own experience, your thoughts, your wisdom. . . . They teach you there's a boundary line to music. But, man, there's no boundary line to art."[3]

Teens who love music might find a career as a musician, conductor, or music teacher.

Musicians themselves fall into many different categories. Some musicians perform solo, either on an instrument or as a vocalist. Others belong to orchestras, or bands, or accompany other performers. So if you like to play an instrument, but aren't sure if you really want to occupy the spotlight, there are still options for you. Being a musician has more possibilities than playing the starring role.

Record producers manage the process of recording music.

If you are interested in working in movies or theater, you might be considering acting. Some actors, usually those with more experience and bigger reputations, are always the stars of the productions they are in. But others play supporting roles, or are part of a chorus, or serve as a supporting cast. Many actors start as extras, with very small roles in movies and plays. Some of them gradually work up to bigger, more important roles.

There are several careers in the performing arts that are less visible. Directors are needed to take a movie or theater script and interpret it for screen or stage. Directors decide on a unifying tone and look for the production and help the actors and designers achieve that vision. Movies also require producers, who handle the business end of performances. Talent scouts and casting agents help directors find the right actors. They also help new actors break into the business. Designers are needed to create sets and costumes, and special effects technicians help create the effects that make movies and theater productions come alive. As with music, theater and movies offer more career options than just the starring role.

## WHO'S WHO IN THE MOVIES

If you've ever watched the end credits of a movie, you know that there are many detailed and diverse job titles in the film industry. Here are descriptions of some of the stranger titles:

- Gaffer: the chief electrician who sets up the lighting on the set.
- Key grip: the person in charge of setting up the equipment—such as cranes, dollies, and platforms—that enable the camera crew to capture the shots they want.
- Best boy: the first assistant to the gaffer or the key grip.
- Foley artist: the person who creates sound effects that aren't captured during actual filming.
- Boom operator: the person who holds the microphone boom near the action to capture spoken dialogue.

## PERFORMING VERSUS DIRECTING

In both music and acting, careers are generally divided between those who actually perform—such as musicians and actors—and those who guide the performers, such as conductors and directors. It's important to consider whether you are more comfortable working in the spotlight or behind the scenes.

> "A film is—or should be—more like music than like fiction. It should be a progression of moods and feelings. The theme, what's behind the emotion, the meaning, all that comes later."[4]
>
> —*Stanley Kubrick, movie director*

Each job in the entertainment industry is better suited to a particular personality type, and each requires its own set of skills and educational path. Whether you think you want to be the lead singer in a rock band, a member of a symphony orchestra, a movie star, or a director with a unique vision for your movies, the following chapters will help you see what it takes to get started in the entertainment industry.

## TEN POPULAR ENTERTAINMENT JOBS

Are you ready to explore which entertainment jobs are good fits for you? This book will cover the following jobs in depth: professional musician, conductor, actor, and director. But first, here is a list of other popular jobs in the field:

1.  **Producer:** A producer manages the funding and organization for making a movie.

2.  **Musical Director:** A musical director directs the musical aspects of a movie or theater production.

3.  **Cinematographer:** Making a movie has many technical aspects. A cinematographer decides how to convey the "look" of the movie, determining camera angles, framing, and effects. In a smaller production, he or she may do the actual filming.

4.  **Composer/Arranger:** A composer writes musical compositions. An arranger picks which instruments or voices will perform a piece of music and how it will sound. Often, one person fulfills both positions.

5.  **Screenwriter:** A screenwriter writes the overall story and the actual lines for the actors in a movie. The story may be an original or an adaptation of an existing story.

6.  **Entertainment Critic:** A critic analyzes and evaluates movies, theater productions, and musical performances for magazines, newspapers, television, or Web sites.

7.  **Stunt Person:** Actors usually do not perform actions in their movies that could be dangerous. A stunt person is specially trained to perform these stunts, usually in place of the actual star.

8. **Publicist:** A publicist handles publicity and media relations for entertainers or productions. A publicist is responsible for developing a positive image for the entertainer or production.

9. **Film and Video Editors:** These people take the raw footage from movies or videos and edit it into the finished product.

10. **Professional Speaker:** Professional speaking is a kind of entertainment. Professional speakers might travel around the world promoting products or services for companies.

The entertainment industry holds abundant career opportunities. Musicians today entertain in new and exciting ways. Conductors continue to inspire and draw out amazing music from bands and choirs. Actors light up the stage and screen with their personal charisma and talent. Directors help pull together all aspects of a performance to make going to the movies a treat. Read on to find out how you can become a part of the action.

Are you interested in an entertainment career? Start gaining experience in school or community performing arts programs!

The music industry offers many careers, from rock guitarist to opera singer.

# WHAT IS A
# PROFESSIONAL
# MUSICIAN?

ne of the best things about the field of music is that it includes many different types of performers and genres. There are so many instruments to play, such as the violin, piano, clarinet, guitar, or drums. Any instrument can be the basis for a musical career. Musicians who play less common instruments, such as the contrabass flute, the piccolo clarinet, the flügelhorn, and the dulcimer, may be in greater demand, since not as many performers know how to play them. Many musicians learn to play several related instruments. The choice of instrument usually determines what kind of music a person plays. For example, dulcimers are better suited for folk music and a contrabass flute is usually played only in a large symphony orchestra. However, today's instruments are often used unexpectedly and in genres of music that previously seemed unsuited to them.

## YOU PLAY *WHAT?*

While most professional musicians play fairly common musical instruments, many unusual instruments are used in public performances or to create certain musical effects. One inventor has created a very unusual musical instrument: the sea organ on the shores of Zadia in the country of Croatia. Thirty-five musical tubes, like organ pipes, are located in a set of marble steps, and the movement of the sea pushes air through the tubes and creates random musical chords and sounds. Other examples of unusual instruments include percussion groups who use "recycled" garbage cans and other found metallic objects to perform percussion works. Some composers have used everyday objects such as cell phone ringtones to create new musical works.

In the case of a singer, his or her vocal range usually falls into four categories. Range refers to the notes—from highest to lowest—the singer can comfortably produce. The highest vocal range is the soprano, followed by the alto. These two ranges are sung by women, although very young boys can also be sopranos. Men's voices fall into the categories of tenor, which is a higher range, and bass. Although a musical composition may include all of these vocal ranges, individual musicians only sing music that falls comfortably within their range. Otherwise they must transpose the music in order to better fit their vocal range.

## NEW USES FOR VOICES

Singers have always found new ways to use their voices to create music. For example, in beatboxing the performer uses his or her lips, voice, and tongue to create percussion sounds or other musical effects. Death growl, or guttural vocals, is a style used in heavy metal rock music, where the singer creates a low, growling tone. Yodeling is a form of singing in which the singer sings a long note that rapidly moves back and forth from a low "chest" voice to a high "head" voice. Yodeling is used by cultures all over the world.

Musicians can be solo performers or part of a group. Pianists and violinists are two of the most common instrumentalists who perform alone. A solo singer is usually accompanied by a guitar, an orchestra, a piano, or a rock band. A singer who is part of a musical theater or opera production will be accompanied by a small orchestra or pit band. Many soloists first started out as part of a musical group. For example, Michael Jackson started with the Jackson 5 before launching a successful solo career.

When it comes to performing with others, an instrumentalist has many choices. He or she may be a member of a symphony orchestra, a rock band, or a jazz ensemble. In a small group, the individual will have more visibility, as well as the opportunity to play solos. In a large group, such as an orchestra, each musician contributes to the group's sound as a whole. An instrumentalist may also work as a session player in recording studios. He or she accompanies other artists during recording sessions. If the instrumentalist is temporarily part of a group recording its music, he or she may work with that group for just a few days.

A vocal performance group can have just a few singers. These include a cappela groups, where each member sings a specific part of the music, or rock bands. Other singers may be part of a large chorus or choir, which performs either by itself or as part of an orchestra, opera, religious service, or musical theater production.

## WHAT IS A PROFESSIONAL MUSICIAN'S WORK ENVIRONMENT?

Musicians work in a variety of environments. Most musicians practice at home or in a designated room or studio. Performances usually take place in a concert hall or theater. While a member of a symphony orchestra may always play in the same concert hall, a member of a country and western band might travel to small clubs, theaters, or venues such as fairs and festivals. Internationally known artists and bands may travel around the country and the world to perform in well-known concert halls, theaters, and even stadiums. Musicians may also perform in churches or temples, as well as at schools, or in parades.

Many musicians, particularly those who are members of a group, live in an urban setting. Smaller musical groups and individual musicians may live anywhere, providing they are willing to travel for shows or concerts. Many rock bands travel on extended tours, which requires living in hotel rooms, personal buses, or trailers for months at a time.

## HOW IS THE JOB MARKET FOR PROFESSIONAL MUSICIANS?

As of 2010, employment for musicians was expected to grow at an average rate compared to other types of jobs, increasing by approximately 8 percent during the decade from 2008 to 2018. In 2008, musicians and singers in the United States held approximately 186,000 jobs. Musicians most likely to have steady, salaried jobs are those who work for religious organizations. Self-employed musicians, on the other hand, will experience slower job growth.[1]

A typical musician may make as much as $60 an hour or as little as $8 an hour. The median wage for a musician in 2008 was approximately $20 an hour. Headliners, such as rock stars or well-known classical musicians, usually earn much, much more. However, musicians are paid only for the time they perform. Hours of unpaid practice and preparation go into one hour on stage.[2]

## A PROFILE OF A PROFESSIONAL MUSICIAN

What is it really like to work as a professional musician? According to Tim Ost, drummer for the Minnesota-based rock

Many musicians make a living by giving music lessons or teaching music in schools.

band Orange Whip, a typical day for a rock musician is more likely to be a typical night. Like most rock bands, Orange Whip does most of its performances in the evenings and on weekends. Once in a while, the band may have a daytime gig, playing for corporate parties, fairs, or street parties. This schedule makes it possible for Ost to be an at-home dad to his kids and to supplement his band income by giving drum lessons during the day.

Ost didn't pursue a college degree in music. He felt that performance experience and practice were much more important to his success as a musician. He approached music seriously during high school, joining marching band and a competitive drum line. He also took every opportunity he could to play in theater productions, rock bands, and regular school band. There were good gigs and bad gigs, and he played with many different bands before Orange Whip.

## THE MUSICIAN AS TEACHER

Because many musicians have little job security and often find themselves facing long periods with no available work, they are likely to be music teachers as well. Talented musicians may teach, either in their own homes or through a music school or organization. The better known a musician is, the more likely he or she will be able to attract students. Many musicians feel that by teaching, they can play a role in encouraging new generations of musicians.

Ost feels that the best thing about his job is the ability to make a living doing something he is passionate about while still being able to spend time with his family. He says the most difficult aspect of the job has been the long years of honing skills and the constant practicing. He also spent a long time playing with many different bands and improving his playing to get to a point where he was part of band that could book well-paying gigs and appearances in popular venues.

Ost's advice to anyone who wants a career as a musician is, "Take every single opportunity to play that you can, no matter what it is. Play any kind of gig, even if you feel threatened, or afraid, or think you can't do it."[3]

# A DAY IN THE LIFE OF A PROFESSIONAL MUSICIAN

Most musicians perform in the evening and often late into the night, especially on weekends. During the day, a musician may teach lessons to supplement his or her income, teach classes at a school or college, or hold a nonmusical day job. Time may also be spent practicing, either at home for a solo musician or at a studio or concert hall for a member of a large orchestra. Daytime rehearsals may be necessary for musicians accompanying a theater or ballet group. Musicians on tour spend part of the day traveling from venue to venue. Studio musicians or those with steady performance schedules tend to work a more normal schedule during the day, with evenings and weekends free.

## A STRESSFUL CAREER

Being a professional musician is a stressful career. Most musicians do not have steady, year-round work with a set salary. The work they do get may be part-time or intermittent. This may add stress to everyday life in terms of making enough money to live on, as well as the stress of having to constantly seek new musical jobs. Physically, musicians may suffer from too much exposure to smoke and dim lighting in places like nightclubs. They can also suffer injuries such as carpal tunnel syndrome from years of practice and playing or hearing loss from prolonged exposure to loud noise.

# TOP FIVE QUESTIONS ABOUT BECOMING A PROFESSIONAL MUSICIAN

1. *How difficult is it to start a career as a musician?*

   Being a musician is a highly competitive job. It takes dedication to practice and improve your musical technique, as well as perseverance in the face of rejection.

2. *How do I know if I have what it takes to be a professional musician?*

   Your music teacher can evaluate how well you play an instrument or sing, and by participating in competitions and performing whenever possible, you will begin to know if you have the necessary talent and dedication.

3. *What do I need to do now to work toward a music career?*

   Practice your instrument or sing as much as possible. You want to be better than your competition.

4. *How hard is it to make a living as a musician?*

   It is difficult to make a living solely through music. Most musicians have other jobs as well. But, if you are very talented and dedicated, you may be able to find a steady position with a musical group or become a headlining performer.

A violinist can work as a solo artist, as part of an orchestra or music group, or as an instructor.

5. **What classes should I take while I'm still in high school?**

In addition to taking classes in music history and theory, if possible, you should take private lessons in your preferred instrument. Classes in communications and English will be helpful, as they can help you learn about expressing emotions and ideas creatively. Public speaking or speech classes can also help you build self-confidence.

Joining your high school choir is a great way to see if you enjoy performing in front of audiences.

# WOULD YOU MAKE A GOOD PROFESSIONAL MUSICIAN?

So what does it take to be a professional musician? The most obvious answer is that you need to love making music, and you need to be proficient either on an instrument or using your singing voice. For most people, musical proficiency usually begins before they reach high school. They might begin as early as six or seven years old on the piano or violin but as late as middle school for band instruments.

## KNOW MUSIC

In addition to being able to play an instrument or sing well, a good musician will also be interested in and knowledgeable about many different types of music. Even if you want to be a rock guitarist or an opera singer, education in different forms of music and musical composition, as well as the history and development of musical styles, will help you gain a background in music as a whole. This will help you perform and understand distinct styles of music. Even a rock guitarist can benefit from familiarity with classical music styles, if only to build off those styles to create a personal musical style. Don't limit yourself by focusing on only one kind of music.

## DEDICATION TO YOUR MUSIC

Above all, being a musician requires talent, a love of music, and a commitment to practicing. Talent is important, since some people, no matter how much they love singing or playing the piano, will never have the sufficient skills or ability to perform professionally. If you don't love music or the idea of devoting most of your time to practicing and improving, then perhaps a music career is not for you. Improving your musical skills will require taking lessons and a lot of time spent practicing.

# CHECKLIST

Is a career as a professional musician a good fit for you? Discover if you've got what it takes with this checklist.

- *Do you play an instrument or sing well? Have you had professional lessons?*

- *Are you willing and able to spend hours every day practicing?*

- *Are you fascinated with many different styles of music, even if you are particularly drawn to just one type?*

- *Will you take advantage of every opportunity to play solo or perform in a group, as well as entering competitions for young musicians?*

- *Are you willing to accept the fact that your income might be low or uncertain, even once you are a professional musician, and that you may have to do other things to supplement your income?*

- *Do you love both playing and listening to music?*

*If you answered yes to most of the questions in the above checklist and feel that you do have what it takes to be a professional musician, get started now. The music industry always needs talented new performers. But if you answered no to more answers, don't worry. There are plenty of steps you can take now to improve and get ready for your career.*

# HOW TO GET THERE

### TAKE LESSONS

The most important part of musicianship is to take private lessons with a professional musician. Your instructor should preferably have performance experience and be able to provide performance opportunities for you. While musicians who aspire to be in rock or pop bands may not have as much formal training as a classical pianist or a violinist, a teacher can help them develop skills, too.

### CLASSES TO TAKE

If your high school has a large enough music department, you may be able to take classes in music theory, music history, and music appreciation. These will help you build the musical skills to be a versatile musician. If you don't have these opportunities, try to research music on your own. Since many rock band

## EARLY TRAINING

Many students get their first taste of learning a musical instrument in elementary school or even earlier. Some schools offer short-term lessons in violin or piano as part of their music curriculum. Many children have participated in lessons through the Suzuki Method, developed by Shinichi Suzuki, a violinist and educator who felt that every child could learn music at an early age as easily as they could learn languages. According to Suzuki, "Musical ability is not an inborn talent but an ability which can be developed. Any child who is properly trained can develop musical ability, just as all children develop the ability to speak their mother tongue. The potential of every child is unlimited."[1] Many professional musicians got their start through Suzuki's methods.

performers often write their own music, music theory classes can teach you how to write down the music. Some schools may even offer classes in composing music using computer software. Get to know the band or choir directors at your school. Do your best to impress them with your dedication to your music. They may be able to connect you with more musical opportunities outside of school.

In addition to music classes, classes in math can be helpful for musicians who write their own music, since the beats and time signatures of music are based on fractions. Creative writing classes are a good option for musicians who would like to write their own lyrics. Communications classes will also be beneficial, because music is all about communicating emotions and ideas.

## *PERFORM*

One of the best ways to build performance skills is to participate in as many different types of performances as possible. In addition to school concerts with the established bands and choruses, you can be part of the pit band in a theater, take part in a talent show, play in a pep band, perform at a religious service, or even form a band with friends. Any performance experience will help you gain skills and make it easier to perform in public and audition with less stage fright. You can also look for summer music camps that will help you gain experience.

## *KEEP PRACTICING!*

Finally, the best thing any musician can do is practice. Practice the music your teacher assigns to you and other

Musicians learn to read, and often compose, music by
taking lessons or classes.

types of music as well. Experiment with widening your musical knowledge and style by trying different types of music. Above all, be willing to devote hours of your time to perfecting your ability to play your instrument or sing. Practice will help you improve both your technique and the quality of your performance.

## WHAT ABOUT COLLEGE?

If you are interested in becoming a professional classical musician or a music teacher at a school, you will need a degree in music performance. In addition to providing the skills and credentials you need to fulfill your career goals, this level of education will give you the opportunity to study with successful professional musicians. They may also have connections with other people in the industry that they can share with you. Music conservatories at the college level are very competitive, however, and high grades may not be enough to get in. You will have to audition, and only the most skilled musicians are accepted. Research the universities you are interested in before you apply. Find out the reputation of their music departments and faculty.

### COLLEGE STATS

A good music college may be difficult to get into, but the benefits can be great. At the Berklee College of Music in Boston, Massachusetts, only 30 percent of those who apply to the college are accepted and admitted. But of those who graduate from Berklee, 80 percent work in the music industry, and 176 Berklee alumni have received Grammy Awards.[2]

A career as a musician requires talent, willingness to practice, and a love for music.

Musicians who are more interested in rock, folk, or pop music most likely will not require a degree to advance in their field. They may find that performance experience and practice are more valuable. However, the background gained through college-level music study is always useful, and the ability to teach later on in a school setting is a valuable skill.

In addition to leading an orchestra in concert, a conductor organizes the musicians, interprets the music, and runs rehearsals.

# WHAT IS A CONDUCTOR?

**Y**ou may not have paid very much attention to them when you've watched concerts, but what keeps symphony orchestras, dance bands, or school choruses playing or singing together? Conductors!

The conductor controls how a particular piece of music is played and is the most important member of a musical group. Whether it's a marching band, an orchestra, a dance band, a choral group, or a small string ensemble, the conductor sets the beat of the music. Using his or her hands, a small baton, or both, the conductor lets the musicians know when to start playing and how loud to play. The conductor is responsible for evoking a certain feeling in the music through tempo and volume. The conductor must be able to think of the piece of music as a whole but still pay attention to the parts that create the entire sound. No two conductors will interpret a piece of music in the same way.

In addition to conducting a group in performance, conductors run rehearsals. They also schedule special sectionals, where one instrumental or vocal part rehearses alone.

## A FAMOUS CONDUCTOR

Sometimes a conductor becomes a household name, almost as famous as a rock star or a singer. Arthur Fiedler, who conducted the Boston Pops for 50 years, was one such conductor.[1] He started as a member of the Boston Symphony Orchestra as a violinist, pianist, organist, and percussionist. He initiated a series of free, outdoor concerts in Boston as a way to bring music to as many people as possible. Under Fiedler's direction, the Boston Pops made more recordings than any other orchestra in the world. More than 50 million copies of the Pops albums, singles, cassettes, and CDs have been sold.[2] In 1977, Fiedler was awarded the Presidential Medal of Freedom at the White House, and he received many other awards and honorary degrees in his lifetime.[3]

35

They are responsible for auditioning new members for the group. Conductors have to be able to relate well with their performers, which can be difficult when there are many different temperaments at work. Conductors may also be called upon to interact with the public and assist with fund-raising and administration.

It may seem odd that a conductor may be equally as famous and respected as a musician when the conductor does not play a single note of music during a performance. However, he or she "plays" music by controlling the sounds of the performers—the entire orchestra group is the instrument! A conductor is usually also proficient on at least one instrument, often the piano, as well as being familiar with many others. School band conductors often need to be familiar with a variety of instruments so that they can teach students how to play them.

## WHAT IS A CONDUCTOR'S WORK ENVIRONMENT?

A local conductor may choose to work in a school setting, for a local symphony orchestra or chorus, or at a church or community center, ensuring that he or she will work somewhat regular hours in one location. Symphony orchestra conductors are likely to have a rehearsal space in one building and a regular concert hall for performances, although they may occasionally travel for performances or even perform outdoors. A conductor who works in a music school or university is likely to have extensive facilities for rehearsals, teaching, and performing.

Arthur Fiedler made a name for himself as conductor
of the Boston Pops.

The leader of a world famous orchestra or chorus, such as the Vienna Boys Choir or the Boston Pops, may travel more extensively, either within the country or around the world. Such conductors perform in a variety of settings, mostly concert halls and auditoriums as well as outside or at historic locations.

## HOW IS THE JOB MARKET FOR CONDUCTORS?

As with most jobs that focus on music, a conductor position is not easy to find. As the operating costs for symphony orchestras rise and their audiences dwindle, positions are even fewer. In the last few decades, the number of orchestras in the United States has risen only slightly. This means that for people who graduate from music school and expressly want to become conductors, there will be fewer jobs and more competition for those jobs. The number of available jobs is not growing as fast as the number of conductors graduating from music schools. Conducting jobs are more readily available in religious organizations such as churches and temples. The number of people working as music conductors, directors, or composers in the United States was approximately 53,600 in 2008 and will only grow to approximately 59,000 by 2018, a 10 percent increase.[4] This percentage cannot accommodate the number of graduates with music degrees who wish to become conductors.

Salaries for conductors vary widely depending on the size of the group, its location, and whether the conductor is also a teacher. The average salary for a music conductor in the United States in 2010 was $45,090, but a conductor in New York earned an average wage of $59,970.[5] Of course, a famous conductor earns a much higher salary. In 2006, conductor James Levine, who led both the Boston Symphony Orchestra and the New York Metropolitan Opera, earned a combined salary of $3.5 million, making him the highest-paid conductor in the United States.[6]

## MUSICAL DIRECTOR

Sometimes a conductor is called a musical director, a title that involves an even wider area of responsibility. Musical directors are often found in theater companies. These professionals work closely with the directors of theater performances and handle all musical aspects of the productions. In addition to conducting the pit orchestras during performances, they help audition the singers and teach them their parts. They conduct musical rehearsals for both singers and the orchestra and play piano accompaniment for other rehearsals. They are also responsible for adapting, expanding, or cutting the music, if need be.

Most conductors who lead smaller instrumental or choral groups also supplement their incomes by teaching. Those who work in secondary or college level schools usually teach both private instrumental lessons and general music classes.

## A PROFILE OF A CONDUCTOR

Schools offer some of the best job opportunities for conductors. School music directors are able to work with kids and explore many different types and styles of music. They also have the advantage of steady employment and regular pay. But what is it really like to conduct a school band program? According to David Aines, band director at Conval High School in Peterborough, New Hampshire, music is just one part of a typical day. Aines's day usually begins at 6:00 a.m. He typically does administrative work until school starts at 7:20. In addition to conducting band rehearsal every day, he also teaches wind ensemble and instrument lessons. One night a week, Aines leads a jazz band rehearsal. Additionally, depending on the time of year, he may be leading performances at sporting events, festivals, and parades.

## NOT ALWAYS A SERIOUS JOB

Musician Victor Borge was known as a great pianist and a great conductor, as well as a comedian. His comedy act included conducting an orchestra and sending a violinist off the stage for allegedly playing a wrong note, then moving the rest of the players around while they were still playing. He was also known for holding notes for an unnaturally long time and scattering pieces of his music or tearing them in half. Borge's comedy brought classical music to people who might not have been interested otherwise.

Aines notes that to teach at a public school, a degree in music or music education is required. But, he adds, "Experience is the best education. Books are great, but doing the job teaches more. Being open to learning from any source, especially kids, is really important."[7]

Aines believes that the most difficult aspects of the job have nothing to do with music, since a teacher has to contend with general school tasks such as standardized testing, disciplinary measures, and educational requirements that come from the school board and the state. Often the administrative work leaves teachers feeling like there isn't enough time to do what needs to be done. As for the benefits of the job, Aines says, "The best thing about my job is the kids. Even after 35 years they still amaze me and I learn from them all the time."[8]

His advice to students interested in a music conducting or music education career is that they should let the career choose them. "[M]y advice to a high school student is, if it draws you, do it. It can be the most rewarding experience of your life."[9]

## A DAY IN THE LIFE OF A CONDUCTOR

A typical day for a conductor varies widely, depending on whether he or she conducts an established orchestra, a musical theater production, or in a school setting. For conductors outside of schools, days are spent looking after the business aspects of his or her performing group, dealing with finances and publicity. A conductor may also audition potential new performers, choose new music, and put together new performances. Regular rehearsals will take place, especially if new music needs to be learned. Performances most often take place in the evening, but there may be weekend matinees or special performances that are

## A MAN'S WORLD?

During the early twentieth century, all-women orchestras were common in the United States and Europe, but after World War II (1939–1945), there were fewer opportunities for women as professional conductors. The industry was male dominated, and many women were either not allowed or unwelcome in most orchestras. It wasn't until the 1980s that women began to have more success as conductors.[10]

According to Anita Mercier in "Pioneers of the Podium," "[Female conductors today] have the opportunity to train, compete, and prove themselves, and they can look to older women in the field as role models. Today women can step up to the podium with more support, self-confidence, and prospects for success than ever before in history. But there are still far fewer women than men choosing to make a career of conducting, and it remains a male-dominated field."[11]

held during the day. A conductor may also have to attend parties or media events before or after performances. A conductor in a school setting usually gives student lessons and participates in administrative duties for the school. Summers and vacations may offer more time for purely musical pursuits.

Conductors sometimes find jobs at churches or schools.

# TOP FIVE QUESTIONS ABOUT BECOMING A CONDUCTOR

1. *What specific interests or skills might make me a good conductor?*

   In addition to being a good musician, you need to be able to work with other people and create a team of musicians. You need to know enough about other instruments, besides your own, to be able to work with other players. You should also know how to make a musical composition evocative and communicate moods and meanings.

2. *How hard will it be for me to find a job as conductor?*

   Being a conductor is a very competitive career because there are more people who want jobs as conductors than there are jobs. It will be very difficult to achieve a position as the conductor of a big, well-known symphony, but easier to conduct on the high school or college level, or in smaller community groups.

## MAESTRO

You may have heard the word *maestro* associated with famous conductors, but what does it really mean? Maestro, an Italian word that means master or teacher, is a title of respect given to a master musician, composer, or conductor. While it is often used for a conductor, it can refer to anyone in music, art, or even literature, who is extremely accomplished.

3. *What do I need to be doing now if I'm interested in conducting?*

   In addition to learning your own musical instrument very well, you should practice working with small groups of musicians and try conducting them whenever possible. Most music teachers will allow students to try conducting in a classroom setting.

4. *What classes should I take?*

   Classes in music theory and history as well as private lessons in your instrument will be the most helpful. Classes in communications, English, and even psychology and history are also good choices.

5. *Do I need to be a certain type of person to be a good conductor?*

   You need to be able to work well with others, even difficult people, and be able to create a feeling of unity while leading a group. If you get along well with other people and find it easy to work with people in a group, you may have what it takes to be a conductor.

A good conductor needs both communication and music skills.

# WOULD YOU MAKE A GOOD CONDUCTOR?

So you think that conducting sounds like a cool career, or perhaps you're already a musician and you wonder if you could also be a conductor? Most conductors don't start out at a young age thinking they want to be conductors. Instead, they might work as musicians or study music and find they have an aptitude for, or an interest in, conducting.

## CONDUCTORS ARE MUSICIANS FIRST

To be a conductor or a musical director, the most important skill is to be a musician first. Conductors are usually formally trained in one particular instrument, but they also need formal training on the keyboard. As a conductor, you'll need to have all the same skills and training as a musician: the discipline necessary to practice an instrument, familiarity with many different types of music, knowledge of music theory and history, and an understanding of musical compositions and arranging. In addition, you'll need to be familiar with each of the different instruments in a band or orchestra, and even a rudimentary knowledge of how to play each one.

## PEOPLE SKILLS

A conductor must also have people

### CONDUCTOR-LESS ORCHESTRAS

There have been musical experiments with "conductor-less" orchestras. In the Communist Soviet Union in 1922, an orchestra was assembled with the belief that no one person should have ultimate control over the other musicians, and that conducting should be done by a committee. The biggest problem with this approach was in maintaining and changing tempos, since no one person was allowed to keep the tempo for the entire group.

Conductor Yu Long directs his orchestra in Shanghai.

skills. If you are good at getting along with other people, feel comfortable in the role of a leader, and like helping others achieve their goals, you will be well suited for the job. Conductors must be good at resolving arguments between people and in dealing with difficult personalities. Good communication skills will also be useful in maintaining relationships on the business side of the job. That also helps with publicity and fund-raising or dealing with school administrations. Business skills are useful in handling the financial side of musical groups. Above all, you need to love music and be committed to achieving and maintaining a high level of musical performance, both in yourself and in the musicians you lead.

## CHECKLIST

Can you see yourself conducting a band or an orchestra?
See if you have a conductor within you, using this checklist.

- *Do you play an instrument well and also have professional training in that instrument and on the keyboard?*

- *Do you have the discipline to practice a variety of instruments daily, perhaps for hours, to perfect your skills?*

- *Are you interested in many types of music, even if you like one particular type the best?*

- *Do you want to compose or arrange music?*

- *Do you feel comfortable being a leader?*

- *Do you have strong communication skills?*

- *Are you willing to start as a musician, perhaps with low or uncertain pay, and work your way up to leading a professional musical group?*

- *Do you love playing and listening to music?*

*If you answered yes to most of the questions, you may be on your way to becoming a conductor! However, if you don't have all these skills yet, don't worry. There is still plenty of time for you to develop them.*

# HOW TO GET THERE

## *LEARN, PRACTICE, AND PERFORM*

You're probably already playing an instrument, but it's important to take lessons with a professional musician and practice to improve your skills. You should also participate in as many performance groups as you can. As a member of a performance group, you can learn about how a band operates and how each individual instrument contributes to the sound as a whole.

Many high school music teachers allow students who are thinking of pursuing music professionally to practice conducting in front of a group. Some teachers may even let a student conduct a piece during a concert. Your music instructor

### THE BIG BAND ERA

Bands of the big band era of the 1930s and 1940s played jazz and swing music and usually had 20 to 25 musicians.[1] Many of the big bands were known by the name of the bandleader, who created the group. The bandleader was essentially the conductor but often a star performer on a specific instrument as well. Bands such as Benny Goodman, Glenn Miller, Count Basie, and Tommy Dorsey were household names, and these men both led the group and soloed on their own particular instrument. The musicians in the band often changed, but the conductor remained.

At the height of their popularity, these bands toured the country and made recordings. It was up to the bandleader to maintain discipline and keep the group together, as well as keep the band's signature sound or style consistent through changes in band membership. Some big bands still tour today.

Conducting your high school marching band is a great way to see if this field is right for you.

can teach you the rudiments of conducting for a certain musical beat and how to cue different sections and control the dynamics of the group. If your school music department allows music students to form small ensembles, such as a wind ensemble, a brass ensemble, or a small choral group, you could assemble a group and conduct it. If your school has a big enough music department, you should also take classes in music theory, music composition, and music history.

## GO TO CONCERTS

Take every opportunity to attend concerts. At a concert, pay close attention to how the conductor leads the group. Each conductor has his or her own personal style. Some conduct with large arm movements. Others prefer a more controlled, low-key approach. Some use a baton while others use only their hands. By studying different techniques, you will be able to see how these conductors control their group and decide what approach works best for you.

## NONMUSIC CLASSES

In addition to music, classes in communications and English are useful for personal interaction and to understand the moods and nuances of creative works and how to evoke them. Participation in school clubs where you can take a leadership role will also be helpful in developing leadership and communication skills.

## WHAT ABOUT COLLEGE?

Since most students don't start out thinking they will become conductors, most colleges and universities don't have a conducting major. Usually students major in music—taking courses in composition, arranging, and orchestration with an eye toward conducting. They may also have the opportunity to study with a professor who conducts a university chorus or orchestra. There are also training programs and intern opportunities for conducting.

Being a successful conductor involves three specific skills: technique, performance, and conducting. Technique involves being able to sight-read and transpose music easily and to have a working knowledge of every instrument. Performance requires understanding specific musical styles and structures and how best to perform them. Conducting itself is the ability to control the group and produce the appropriate sounds and effects with it. These skills are most easily acquired through university-level musical training and practice.

It was once thought that you couldn't teach someone to be a conductor, which is another reason why many music schools don't offer a program specifically for conducting. However, that opinion is changing. Some

## KEEPING TRACK

A conductor of a choral group, orchestra, music theater production, or ballet has to keep track of many different instrumental parts. The conductor usually has something called the conductor's score, which shows all of the instrumental and choral parts on one page. Reading one of these scores is challenging, especially since the conductor is also keeping time and bringing instrumentalists and singers in on cue.

music schools, such as the Paris Conservatory, now allow students to specifically study conducting. Graduation from one of these programs makes it much easier to get a job as a conductor in an established institution or group.

College-level courses in languages are also useful, particularly for choral conductors whose groups may sing music in many different languages. Knowledge of history, both musical and general, is helpful, as are college-level courses in communications and even psychology classes for dealing with musicians and the community.

Conductors usually train as musicians first.

Hollywood celebrities such as Brad Pitt and Angelina Jolie make up only a small percentage of working actors.

# WHAT IS AN ACTOR?

You see actors all the time in movies, tabloid headlines, and magazines. But Hollywood actors represent only a small portion of working actors. Actors may work on the live stage, in an operatic production, or in summer stock theater. They may perform a role in an ongoing television or movie series that lasts for several years. Actors also do voice-overs and television commercials; they work as stand-ins, body doubles, and stunt people.

Acting may sound easy and glamorous, but in reality, it can be demanding and tiring work. First, acting involves getting a role, which requires auditioning for the director and other people involved in the production. Film actors may take screen tests to see how they come across on camera. Once they have a job, actors must memorize lines as well as cues; they must be able to follow the director's instructions as to how the role should be interpreted.

This involves many hours of rehearsal with the entire production group, as well as time alone for memorization. Television actors may have an advantage in that their lines are often scrolled on teleprompters off camera, and radio actors usually read their lines from a script. However, they still must study to understand the nuances of their roles and how to convey the emotions and motivations the director wants to see. Actors must be experts at using their voices, gestures, and expressions to convey those emotions. Stage actors, who may perform the same role for months or even years, must also be able to keep their performances fresh and interesting after many, many repetitions.

Actors who work as body doubles, stunt people, or stand-ins are usually chosen because they resemble the lead actor whom they will be standing in for, often in situations that require nudity or dangerous stunts. Extras are actors who perform nonspeaking roles, usually as part of a background setting for the leading actors in a film or stage production. They may sing as a chorus in a musical production, but generally they do not appear in the credits by name.

## WHAT IS AN ACTOR'S WORK ENVIRONMENT?

Very few actors are able to work in the same place for very long. Even a successful Broadway show might last for only a few months or a few years. Stage actors may be able to live in a large city such as New York or London and find acting jobs regularly, acting in the city during the winter months and going to stock theaters in the suburbs during the summer. Film actors often maintain homes in Los Angeles, California, where the film industry is centered.

Acting itself may be done on an inside soundstage, movie studio, or theater. Some actors may also work in theme parks or resorts. Filming on location often means working outside in any kind of weather or terrain, in conditions that may be difficult or uncomfortable. Acting often involves unusual hours. Most theater productions take place at night, when audiences have the free time to see them. Television and radio work may have more regular hours, but actors in a television series generally work 13-week cycles and they are in the studio for many hours at a time. Radio actors may be able to prerecord their performances, but in some cases, they too have to perform according to a schedule of when listeners are most likely to be tuned in. A movie actor works according to the requirements of a particular scene,

Actors must rehearse for a performance.

which may mean early-morning or late-night filming sessions, or filming in adverse weather conditions.

## HOW IS THE JOB MARKET FOR ACTORS?

Because of the glamour and money associated with those at the top of the profession, acting is highly competitive. Actors have to deal with long periods of unemployment, intense competition for roles, and rejections after auditioning. Like musicians, actors may have to supplement their incomes by holding side jobs.

### UNIONS

Many actors in both film and theater benefit from belonging to unions, which may help guarantee a minimum wage for their work and protect their interests. The Actors' Equity Association is a professional union for actors in theater and other live productions, as well as stage managers, some directors, and choreographers. The Screen Actors Guild (SAG) is a similar organization for screen actors, directors, and producers.

According to the US Bureau of Labor Statistics, from 2008 through 2018, acting as a job is expected to grow as fast as the average for all jobs (approximately 11 percent), but competition will continue to be tough as there are always more actors than there are roles. In 2008, there were approximately 56,000 actors in the United States, and that number is expected to grow to almost 64,000 by 2018.[1]

A typical actor earns an average of approximately $16 an hour, but some actors make as little as $9 an hour and others may make as much as $29 an hour. Extremely successful actors, usually working in movies, may earn much more than that, with high-profile, well-known actors making millions of dollars per movie. However, of all the actors who belong to the Screen Actors Guild (SAG), approximately 50 out of 100,000 can expect to make such high salaries.[2]

## A PROFILE OF AN ACTOR

Ken Sheldon, a full-time writer and performer from New Hampshire, has appeared on radio, television, and the stage. He has also created an award-winning variety show called Frost Heaves. Sheldon has considerable experience as an actor, particularly with the Peterborough Players summer stock theater in Peterborough, New Hampshire.

Sheldon points out that although acting is hard work and actors usually don't make a lot of money, the best thing about acting is that, "it's fun pretending to be someone else, learning how to speak, move, and even think differently than you normally do. Actors are generally very friendly, welcoming, and fun to be around."[3] While Sheldon didn't pursue acting in college, he does feel that his background in English and writing has been helpful. Most of his training came from watching the talented professional actors of the Peterborough Players.

Sheldon's advice to someone interested in an acting career? "As with anything else you are interested in, see if you can get involved in some way that will give you a taste for what the career would be like."[4]

# A DAY IN THE LIFE OF AN ACTOR

Most actors on the stage will do most of their work at night, when they perform. They may spend the day at a regular job, auditioning for new roles, or rehearsing for an upcoming show. Until the performance is about to happen, they may do most of their rehearsing during the day. With steady, long-term roles on Broadway or for touring shows, rehearsals are minimal. Most work occurs during evening and weekend performances, although traveling shows require daytime travel from one venue or city to another. Television and movie actors may shoot scenes during the day or at night, depending on the needs of the show. They may work extremely long hours for a few months, followed by a long break. All actors may go for long periods of time with no work at all and will spend their days auditioning and looking for new roles.

"Never forget acting is a big fat trick we play on an audience. You're standing [in] a set. It's not real, but it's real enough, and the audience is willing enough to suspend disbelief that there you are in the setting and you're wearing somebody else's clothes that have been designed. So it's the actor's job to figure out what his character wants and to do something that's similar to that so that it looks like you're making it up as you go along."[5]

—*William H. Macy, film actor*

Sometimes, actors must step outside their comfort zones to perform roles.

# TOP FIVE QUESTIONS ABOUT BECOMING AN ACTOR

1. *How competitive is acting, and what are my chances of making it as an actor?*

   Acting is extremely competitive, both on stage and in movies. You have to be willing to work your way up, endure periods of unemployment, and live without a steady or secure income, at least at first. It takes perseverance and the ability to move beyond rejections.

2. *What kinds of acting jobs are there?*

   Actors can work on stage, in movies, and on television, and also as voice-over artists and stunt people. They can also work in large theaters or studios, or in local community productions.

## ACTORS AREN'T THE ONLY ONES

Acting skills may also be necessary or at least helpful in a variety of other occupations related to movies and theater. For example, announcers, dancers and choreographers, and musicians who work in theater settings can benefit from acting skills. And if you want to work in theater or movies, but don't see yourself as an actor, there are many related jobs, such as costume designer, makeup artist, and set designer, which are just as vital to productions as actors.

3. *What should I do now if I'm interested in becoming an actor?*

Take acting lessons if possible, but the most important thing is to participate in as many different types of performances as possible, including plays, musical theater, and independent films.

4. *Should I go to college or just start working as an actor immediately?*

Most successful actors have postsecondary training, so it is wise to attend college. College also provides you with more opportunities for participating in plays and movies. You can always audition for roles while you are still in school.

5. *Is it possible to make a living just as an actor?*

It is possible, but difficult, to make a living only as an actor. Most actors also have side jobs or teach theater in school settings.

Part of being an actor is preparing for and going to auditions.

# WOULD YOU MAKE A GOOD ACTOR?

So you've read all about what it's like to be an actor, and you think it's something you'd like to do. But what does it really take to be an actor? What should you do to get started?

## LOVE THE STAGE

Acting can be grueling and frustrating. It may take years to achieve any success, so the most important thing is that you love to perform in plays and be on stage. Even if you're sometimes nervous and suffer from stage fright, you can't imagine not acting. Maybe you've been making up stories and acting them out since you were a little kid, and once you started school you tried out for every school drama production that came along.

### STAGE AND SCREEN

While acting may seem like acting no matter what kind of production you're in, there are major differences between acting on stage and acting in a movie. Stage actors may need to use exaggerated gestures and speech in order to portray their characters, but this same style of acting appears comical on film. Film actors must be subtle and realistic in their performances. They may also be less able to build up an emotional continuity, since scenes may be filmed out of sequence or in small, disconnected pieces. Stage actors can use audience reaction to tailor their performance, but screen actors don't have this advantage, since they can't gauge the reactions of their audience.

## CREATIVITY AND SPECIAL TALENTS

Actors are creative people, so it helps if you are talented artistically. Perhaps you like to write, or you can sing and dance or draw or paint. Any kind of creative endeavor that

## ADVICE FROM A PROFESSIONAL

"I thought being an actor meant being famous. But most actors aren't recognizable. . . . There are so many actors that make a living by doing support work on shows. I was that person for many years. For me to stay in this business, it had to be okay if I was never recognized. I learned that I loved the craft of acting more than the idea of being famous. It can take a very, very, very long time to succeed in this business and my best piece of advice is to not give up. You have to motivate yourself and just keep going. . . . I had a teacher once who said, 'If you can think of anything else you are passionate about besides acting, do that. Your life will be better for it.' I actually think that might be good advice. I couldn't come up with anything, so I moved to LA."[1]

—Jenna Fischer, Pam Beesly on The Office

helps you show emotion will be helpful as an actor. You need to be able to convey emotions on stage and interact with other actors so that your audience believes you are really the character. Communication skills are also very important. And you should have a good speaking voice that is loud and clear. The ability to memorize lines is also important. Most actors spend a good deal of time memorizing their lines.

Do you have an unusual talent that might be useful in an acting career? Singing and dancing are useful, but how about skating, juggling, being a mime, or acrobatics? Have you done any modeling? You never know when an unusual skill may help you get a role.

# CHECKLIST

Do you have what it takes to become an actor? Answer the questions in this checklist to find out!

- *Have you always liked to perform in front of other people?*

- *Are you a creative person, and do you know how to express yourself and your emotions through acting?*

- *Can you read, understand, and memorize lines?*

- *Do you love the theater and enjoy attending theatrical performances?*

- *Do you have the persistence and determination to see you through the long process of finding work and building a career?*

*If you answered yes to most of these questions, a career in acting might be perfect for you. Remember that you can always develop the skills that you lack and with enough determination and hard work, you can achieve your dream of becoming an actor.*

# HOW TO GET THERE

## GET INVOLVED

An actor needs to attend as many theater productions as possible. By watching other actors perform and seeing firsthand what kinds of acting jobs are available, you will

Students interested in an acting career should attend as many theater performances as possible.

get a broad view of what actors do and what kinds of jobs are available. It will also be helpful to talk to people who are involved in professional theater or filmmaking for an inside view of what it's like to be an actor. In addition to attending live theater performances, you should also read plays and become familiar with a wide range of famous theatrical works.

In addition to attending theater productions, you should become involved in as many theater productions as possible, and not just as an actor. These include school productions or community theater performances. Even working as part of the props or lighting crew or helping with costumes and makeup will give you added experience in the field. Many high schools participate in drama festivals. There, the school cast performs a one-act play to be judged against other schools. Some of these festivals give awards to outstanding student actors. Awards like these look good on your résumé. Consider attending theater camps or being an apprentice at a summer stock theater. Participating in amateur filmmaking, perhaps as a volunteer actor, is also a valuable experience.

"Study, find all the good teachers and study with them, get involved in acting to act, not to be famous or for the money. Do plays. It's not worth it if you are just in it for the money. You have to love it."[2]

—*Philip Seymour Hoffman,*
*actor and director*

71

## CLASSES TO TAKE

There are no specific education requirements for becoming an actor. However, very few actors today have no formal training. At the high school level, participate in as many theatrical productions as possible. You should also take classes in English, literature, and communications to study the works of great playwrights and writers. This can teach you how to identify and portray the emotions in works of literature. Classes in psychology will help you understand human emotions, and history classes provide background for a wide range of future roles. If your school offers them, take classes in film, music, and acting. Speech classes can help you practice speaking in front of large groups.

### SAG ADVICE

In the frequently asked question section of The Screen Actors Guild (SAG) Web site, they answer the most common question from aspiring actors: Can I make a living as an actor?

"It may take several years for a beginner to earn a living as a performer. You must have a substantial cushion of savings to fund your quest and/or secure consistent alternate work to support you during the early stages of your career. Even the most talented performers may do everything right and still not end up with acting jobs. Success in this business is an unpredictable combination of talent, training, residence, 'look,' energy, attitude, and the completely uncontrollable factor—luck! You must not take rejection personally! Even a working professional may not earn their income performing in just one medium."[3]

If you can sing, participation in choral groups will be useful. You might also consider professional vocal training. A good vocal teacher will not only help you learn to sing but also to improve your speaking voice. Lessons in singing will give you the ability to read music and to perform in musical theater as well.

## WHAT ABOUT COLLEGE?

It may seem like the best way to become an actor is to simply get out there, audition, and start working. However, these days, most actors are expected to have a college degree in theater arts or dramatic arts. This provides them with a broad background in liberal arts, as well as specific acting skills. Courses in radio and television broadcasting, communications, film, theater, and dramatic literature are all useful. College also provides many opportunities for participating in theatrical productions.

### METHOD ACTING

Some of the most successful actors in the world received their training from the Actors Studio in New York City. For 50 years, the Actors Studio has used a process called "method acting" to teach people how to be great actors. Actors such as Dustin Hoffman, Alec Baldwin, and Robert De Niro have used method acting to perfect their skills. Method acting requires using a variety of techniques to actually *create* the thoughts and emotions of their characters within themselves, whereas classical acting techniques rely on actors using tone of voice and facial expressions to *simulate* the appearance of emotions.

For people who might want to teach drama someday, a graduate college degree may be required. Advanced degrees may involve courses in stage speech and movement, playwriting, stage design, and directing. There are also postgraduate programs and workshops, such as the Actors Studio in New York City, for advanced training.

## FIND AN AGENT

Ultimately, you may also want to find a casting agency, which specializes in providing actors to movie studios. A casting agency fills specified roles, particularly extras in movies. Casting agencies usually accept new clients only when they are looking for specific types of actors, such as small children, senior women, or athletic men, so that they have a variety of actors to provide when a movie studio is seeking a specific type of extra for a scene.

School theater programs are a great way to
gain acting experience.

Directors must be able to work well with many different people.

# WHAT IS A DIRECTOR?

You love movies and the theater, but you don't want to be an actor. You've thought about directing movies, but you don't really know what a director does, other than sit in a chair with his or her name on it and yell

"Action!" or "Cut!" And since theater directors are rarely seen, you have no idea what else they do. So what exactly is a director, and what part does he or she have in making a movie or a play?

Whether in live theater, television productions, or movies, a director has basically the same role—to supervise the performance. A director starts by evaluating and choosing a script, then auditioning and choosing actors for the performance, or in the case of movies, working with casting agents and watching potential actors in screen tests to see how they look on camera and how they interact with each other. The director knows the overall flavor or feeling that he or she wants to evoke.

Once the play or movie is cast, the director works with the actors on their lines and stage movements to bring out that desired feeling. The director conducts rehearsals and works with set and costume designers to achieve the desired "look" of the production. Movie directors also work with designers for setting and costumes, as well as special effects and stunt people. Once the movie begins filming, the director tells the actors what their movements should be and how to deliver their lines. Both theater and movie directors also handle the business side of their productions. They work with producers, financial people, and publicity to ensure the production is ready on time and within a set budget.

Large productions may have many different levels of directors. In addition to the director of the performance, there may be an assistant director who cues performers and technicians, telling them when to make their entrances.

> "I dream for a living."[1]
>
> —*Steven Spielberg, on making movies*

Assistant directors may also direct lighting, sound, or set changes. The director of the performance may report to an executive director, who is the final authority on every factor relating to the production but is usually not present at every rehearsal and spends more time on the business aspects of the production.

## WHAT IS A DIRECTOR'S WORK ENVIRONMENT?

Like actors, directors may work in many different types of settings. New York City is the center of the theater industry, and Los Angeles is the center for the film industry. Theater directors may work in a large Broadway theater or a small summer stock theater, on a college campus, or in a high school as part of their teaching position. A movie director may work on a soundstage in Hollywood or on location anywhere in the world. He or she may operate in difficult conditions, such as remote and primitive areas or in harsh weather.

## HOW IS THE JOB MARKET FOR DIRECTORS?

As with acting, directing positions can be difficult to find, especially at first. And like actors, directors may begin with small hourly wages and earn extremely high salaries once

DIRECTING

Some Hollywood directors such as Martin Scorsese, *left*, and
Steven Spielberg, *right*, make millions of dollars.

they have become established and have proven they can make blockbuster movies or direct successful Broadway shows.

According to the US Bureau of Labor Statistics, in 2008 the average annual salary of a director was just under $65,000. Directors in the motion picture industry generally made higher salaries than those in theater or television. The number of people employed as either directors or producers was approximately 98,000, and that number is expected to rise to 108,000 by 2018. Many directors belong to unions, which may help them negotiate contracts and salaries. Some theater directors receive royalties, or a percentage of profits, based on the number of performances, particularly in smaller theaters. Broadway directors not only receive a set payment amount, but also royalties based on the box office receipts. So, a long-running, popular show may actually pay the director more in royalties than the original contracted fee.[2]

Many directors, particularly those who haven't established a reputation yet, will have to supplement their earnings with other jobs, such as

## THE BIG BUCKS

Which directors are the highest paid in Hollywood? In 2009, director Steven Spielberg made approximately $85 million, while James Cameron made $50 million.[3] That's a big difference from the average film director's salary of $86,000, and part of the reason why people think all directors earn such high salaries.[4]

teaching. Just as with most careers in theater and movies, directing is a competitive market and often produces an unreliable income.

## A PROFILE OF A DIRECTOR

So what is it like to work as a director? Keith Stevens is managing director of the Peterborough Players summer stock theater in Peterborough, New Hampshire. He spends seven months of the year preparing for just five months of shows. His job includes everything necessary to put on the plays: fund-raising, marketing, ticketing, hiring, paying bills, and even sometimes directing the actual performances. "For every actor you see onstage," Stevens notes, "There are four to six people working behind the scenes."[5] Stevens has been trained in all aspects of theater and production, as well as business. He feels it is necessary for a director to know about every part of the theater to be able to understand the technical aspects, the actors, and the business side. Stevens has a master's degree in management with a focus on directing.

Stevens says the best thing about his job is "watching everything come together in a play: actors, tech, design. Knowing that I had something to do with it is a pleasure to me, especially when I watch the audience responding to the play, either perfectly quiet or laughing."[6] Stevens also mentions that it is a very time-consuming job, since the Players puts on a new show every two weeks and there's no break once the season starts. It can be tough to deal with your own exhaustion and that of the people you work with,

## M. NIGHT SHYAMALAN

One of today's most popular movie directors is M. Night Shyamalan. Born in India but raised in the United States, he has been making movies since he was a kid. He has written and directed many popular movies such as *The Sixth Sense* and *Signs*. His movie career started when he was eight years old and he was given a movie camera. Shyamalan was inspired by the work of Steven Spielberg. He wrote, directed, acted in, and raised all the money for his first film, *Praying with Anger* (1992). In 2002, he became the highest paid screenwriter in Hollywood when Disney gave him $5 million to write *Signs* (2002).[9]

especially at times when they don't all get along.

Stevens's advice to students interested in working in the theater is "Get to know the art: acting, design, and directing."[7] He also stresses the importance of a liberal arts education, not just one focused entirely on theater. "The more you know about the world outside you, the more you bring to your art, presenting life on the stage. Live life, and don't just spend 24 hours a day in a dark theater."[8]

## A DAY IN THE LIFE OF A DIRECTOR

Both theater and movie directors may work long days and weekends. Theater directors are more likely to work at night when most people attend the theater, but even movie directors may have to shoot night scenes. A director may spend time in meetings or on the phone with producers and businesspeople. However, the majority of a director's time

M. Night Shyamalan

during production is spent with the actors on stage or the set, creating the performance. Work is generally intensive for a short period of time, and may be followed by periods of unemployment or preparation for the next production.

# TOP FIVE QUESTIONS ABOUT BECOMING A DIRECTOR

1. *What exactly does a director do?*

   A director is responsible for supervising the entire production of a play, television show, or movie. He or she chooses a script, decides how the performance should look and feel, finds and works with actors, while also working with publicity and the business side of the production.

2. *What types of directors are there?*

   Directors work in live theater, radio, television (including commercials), and movies.

3. *Does a director need to be an actor first?*

   It is helpful for a director to be an actor first, so that he or she is familiar with the craft and methods of acting and can better help actors achieve the results they want.

4. *How do I know if I have what it takes to direct?*

   If you love the theater or movies, are interested in acting, and also work well with other people, even when they are difficult, you may have what it takes to be a director. You also need creativity and the ability to determine the mood or message of a play or movie. Good communication skills are also helpful.

5. *What should I be doing now if I want to become a director?*

   You should take every opportunity to act in different kinds of plays. If you can, try directing a play or even an independent film through your school or with friends. If your school participates in drama competitions, become involved.

You can start making your own movies now
using home video equipment.

# WOULD YOU MAKE A
# GOOD DIRECTOR?

**Y**ou think directing sounds like fun, but do you have
what it takes to be a good director of movies or
stage productions? And what type of education and training
will you need to get started and become successful?

## AN ACTING BACKGROUND

Many directors actually start out as actors, before deciding that they prefer to be behind the camera rather than in front. Directors need to have, above all, a love of the theater or the film business. Directing, and building a successful career as a director, can take a long time and be extremely frustrating and competitive. An underlying love of what you're doing will help you persevere.

### CINEMATOGRAPHER

What is the difference between a director and a cinematographer? While the director is responsible for the overall "look" of a movie, he or she needs the help of the cinematographer to bring that look to life. The cinematographer decides how to achieve a specific look through the use of different camera angles, lighting, close-ups or far shots, and filters. The cinematographer is also responsible for managing the camera crew and telling them how to film each scene. When the director and the cinematographer work well together, the movie will usually be made quickly and successfully.

## CREATIVITY AND COMMUNICATION

Has anyone ever told you that you're creative? Creativity and artistic ability are also important skills for a director. A director must look at a script and envision what it could be as a movie or play, then think of creative ways to get that message or mood across to the audience.

## WOMEN DIRECTORS

Women are still underrepresented in the directing profession. Only a few women have ever been nominated for the Best Director category of the Academy Awards. In 2010, Kathryn Bigelow became the first woman to win an Academy Award for best director, for the film *The Hurt Locker*.[1] Sofia Coppola and Penny Marshall are also successful female directors.

Organizations such as Women in Film & Television address issues relating to female directors and other women in the film industry. The American Film Institute (AFI) also offers a Directing Workshop for Women. These organizations promote women as directors.

The ability to communicate well with others is especially useful for a director, who needs to be able to convey to actors what he or she is looking for and trying to achieve in a scene. Actors will want to work with directors who are good at explaining what they want from the actor.

A director may also have to deal with temperamental actors, businesspeople, producers, and other people who are important to the success of a movie or play. How successful the director is at communicating with these people may determine the success of his or her film. As a director, you'll need to cope with many different personality types to ensure that a production runs smoothly. Therefore, in addition to being a good communicator, you'll need to be confident and direct in your negotiations. You must also be self-assured about your vision for the performance, so that it will turn out as you have planned.

Director Kathryn Bigelow won an Academy Award for her film *The Hurt Locker* in 2010.

# CHECKLIST

Do you have the skills to be a director? Find out if you are destined for a career as a director by using the checklist below.

- *Do you love movies and theater?*

- *Are you interested in how performances are shaped to create a particular effect?*

- *Are you interested in telling stories and expressing emotions?*

- *Do you like to analyze particular directors' styles? Do you have firm opinions about what works and what doesn't?*

- *Are you interested in how movies and plays are created?*

- *Are you persistent and willing to work hard for a long time to achieve a successful career as a director?*

*If you answered yes to most of these questions, then you might have a future as a director. If you feel you lack some of the skills listed above, it's okay. With enough hard work and determination, you can still reach your goal.*

# HOW TO GET THERE

## CLASSES TO TAKE

Like actors, aspiring directors can begin by taking classes in English, literature, and communications to study the works of great authors and playwrights and to understand

One way to prepare for a directing career is to watch movies, paying careful attention to the directing choices.

how to identify the meaning in a piece of literature and how emotions are conveyed. Classes in psychology will also be useful both for understanding human emotions and for dealing with other people successfully. If your school has them, take classes in film studies and theater arts, and participate in as many school productions as you can, in any role, such as actor, stagehand, stage manager, or lighting technician.

## LEARN BY EXAMPLE AND EXPERIENCE

If you think you want to become a director, you should also attend as many theater performances and movies as possible. At the performances, pay attention to how the director has shaped the actors' performances to convey a certain mood. When watching a movie, take note of how the director uses elements like color, setting, cinematography, and action to create a mood. Listen to the director's commentary on the DVD of the movie, if available. It is especially helpful to watch multiple movies or performances by a single director until you can start to identify his or her style. If a movie is a remake of an older movie, you can also watch the different versions of the film and take note of how different directors handle them.

"The oldest form of theater is the dinner table. It's got five or six people, new show every night, same players. Good ensemble; the people have worked together a lot." [2]

—Michael J. Fox, actor

Since many directors start out as actors, and because you will ultimately be telling actors how to act in your production, it helps to have acting experience. Participate in theater productions at your school, in your community, or anywhere else where you can learn about how to act.

## GET STARTED

Many schools have film festivals to encourage students to make their own movies. This is a great way to get a feel for directing a movie and all the elements that need to come together. It's easy to make short movies with a home video camera. It will not only give you valuable experience, but also help you build a portfolio of movies to use in

### AMERICAN FILM INSTITUTE

College graduates who have completed a film studies degree at the undergraduate level may decide to go to film school on the graduate level. Programs such as the AFI in Los Angeles offer courses in cinematography, directing, editing, producing, and production design. These schools are extremely competitive, accepting just a few students out of the hundreds who apply, but many famous directors have come out of these programs.

applying to college as a film major. Some schools have classes or programs where students can direct theater productions.

You should seek out opportunities in community theater and film activities in the summer. Working as an apprentice for a summer stock theater will help you become familiar with all aspects of a theater production, as well as provide opportunities for acting. Some colleges offer summer film programs for high school students. You can look for opportunities to volunteer as an actor or extra in a film production.

## WHAT ABOUT COLLEGE?

While many directors start out as actors and may skip college in order to become working actors immediately and gain real-world experience, many colleges have film studies and theater majors that are useful to aspiring directors. A degree from a college will also allow you to work as a director in a high school setting, since teachers must have a degree to be certified to teach. Studying film at the college level not only gives you the chance to take classes about classic films and film history, but also to learn hands-on moviemaking techniques. Most film studies departments have studios where students can learn film production by doing it. You can learn to make your own films and then edit them with filmmaking software. Theater students can study the history of drama and classic plays, as well as learn acting techniques and try their hand at directing a theater production.

College is important, but ultimately, becoming a successful director relies heavily on gaining real-world experience and making connections with people who will help you secure jobs and build a reputation. That is the most difficult aspect of becoming a director. However, having a real love of the job can sustain you in this competitive business.

A director often chooses actors for a play or movie after seeing them audition.

# GET YOUR FOOT IN THE DOOR

The most important thing to remember when you're trying to get your foot in the door of the entertainment industry is that the more experience you have, the better. Whether you play an instrument or sing, want to direct vocal or band groups, or feel acting is your calling, take every opportunity to perform. Join community musical or theater groups, volunteer to take leadership roles directing other musicians or actors, and seek out programs that allow you to intern or volunteer in professional musical groups or theaters. Talk to your high school drama and music teachers about summer programs and camps. The best way to break into entertainment is to get out there and do as much performing as you can.

Additionally, develop a network of people who work in the entertainment industry. You may have met these professional entertainers in school or community settings. Perhaps you can develop relationships as an intern in a theater or musical group. These people may be your key to finding interesting roles or striking up collaborations. As insiders in the business, they may also be able to offer you career tips and put you in contact with even more people in your area of interest. Every new person you meet represents new opportunities for your budding career.

Finally, remember that the entertainment industry is a very competitive field. There are many people who dream of the stage or of directing the next hit movie. True, you might not be the next Lady Gaga or Robert Pattinson, but you do have a chance to work in an industry you love. If you give up before even trying, you will never know what you might be missing. Follow your dream, but realize that you may need to work a second job or take on less visible roles or positions than you have imagined.

Keep taking every opportunity that comes your way. Be open to learning about your profession. With some hard work and a lot of determination, you'll be on your way to a career in the entertainment industry!

# PROFESSIONAL ORGANIZATIONS

Here are some professional organizations that you might want to contact for more information on the jobs in this book.

## PROFESSIONAL MUSICIAN

American Federation of Musicians
www.afm.org

American Guild of Musical Artists
www.musicalartists.org

National Association for Music Education
www.menc.org

## CONDUCTOR

American String Teachers Association
www.astaweb.com

College Band Directors National Association
www.cbdna.org

Conductor's Guild Inc.
www.conductorsguild.org

World Association for Symphonic Bands and Ensembles
www.wasbe.com

## ACTOR

American Theatre Wing
americantheatrewing.org

Drama League
dramaleague.org

National Association of Schools of Theater
www.nast.arts-accredit.org

Screen Actors Guild Young Performers
youngperformers.sag.org

## DIRECTOR

American Film Institute
www.afi.com

Directors Guild of America
www.dga.org

Educational Theatre Association
www.edta.org

# MARKET FACTS

| JOB | NUMBER OF JOBS | GROWTH RATE | |
|---|---|---|---|
| Professional Musician | 186,400 | as fast as average | |
| Conductor | 14,330 | as fast as average | |
| Actor | 56,500 | as fast as average | |
| Director | 98,600 | as fast as average | |

| MEDIAN WAGE | RELATED JOBS | SKILLS |
|---|---|---|
| $21.24 per hour | musical instrument repairers and tuners, musical conductor or director, composer, arranger | musical ability in voice or instrument |
| $45,090 per year | musician, musical theater director, director of music in churches or schools, composer | technical musical ability, ability to interpret music, knowledge of many musical styles |
| $16.59 per hour | producer, announcer, dancer/ choreographer, musician, costume designer | creativity, acting talent, ability to perform |
| $64,430 per year | actor, musical director, managing director, producer | acting skills, ability to work with others, some business skills |

All statistics from the *Bureau of Labor Statistics Occupational Outlook Handbook, 2010–2011 Edition*

# GLOSSARY

**accompany**
To provide a musical background for a singer or other instrument.

**acrobatics**
Gymnastic feats or skills, such as tightrope walking, which require agility and skill.

**apprentice**
A person who works for someone else in order to gain practical experience and learn a trade.

**dulcimer**
An hourglass-shaped instrument, held flat across the lap, with strings that are plucked by the fingers.

**music theory**
The study of harmonics, musical forms, and how music is written.

**portray**
To represent a person or role dramatically on stage, or in the movies.

**primitive**
Simple, unsophisticated, crude; without modern conveniences.

**proficient**
Well-advanced, competent, or skilled.

**soundstage**
A room or building used for filming movies and television shows.

**special effects**
Unusual visual or sound effects in a movie.

**summer stock**
A summer theater, usually located in a resort or suburban area.

**symphony orchestra**
A large orchestra consisting of string, wind, and percussion instruments.

**technique**
The way in which a musician or an actor uses the technical skills of his or her art.

**teleprompter**
A machine that shows an actor's lines, usually for television, located off camera.

**transpose**
To change the key of a musical composition.

**union**
An organization of employees formed to protect their common interests and improve their working conditions.

# ADDITIONAL RESOURCES

## FURTHER READINGS

Field, Sally. *Career Opportunities in the Music Industry*. New York: Ferguson, 2010. Print.

Horn, Geoffrey M. *Writing, Producing, and Directing Movies*. Milwaukee, WI: Gareth Stevens, 2006. Print.

Nathan, Amy. *Meet the Musicians: From Prodigies (or Not) to Pros*. New York: Henry Holt, 2006. Print.

Nathan, Amy. *The Young Musician's Survival Guide: Tips from Teens and Pros*. New York: Oxford U, 2008. Print.

O'Neill, Joseph R. *Movie Director*. Ann Arbor, MI: Cherry Lake, 2010. Print.

Parks, Peggy J. *Careers for the Twenty-First Century: Music*. San Diego, CA: Lucent, 2002. Print.

Rauf, Don. *Virtual Apprentice: Actor*. New York: Ferguson, 2009. Print.

Rauf, Don. *Virtual Apprentice: Pop Musician*. New York: Ferguson, 2008. Print.

Reeves, Lindsey. *Career Ideas for Kids Who Like Music and Dance*. New York: Checkmark, 2007. Print.

Yager, Fred. *Career Opportunities in the Film Industry*. New York: Checkmark, 2009. Print.

## WEB LINKS

To learn more about entertainment jobs, visit ABDO Publishing Company online at **www.abdopublishing.com**. Web sites about entertainment jobs are featured on our Book Links page. These links are routinely monitored and updated to provide the most current information available.

# SOURCE NOTES

## CHAPTER 1. IS AN ENTERTAINMENT JOB FOR YOU?

1. Jorge J. E. Gracia and William Irwin. *Philosophy and the Interpretation of Pop Culture*. Lanham, MD: Rowman & Littefield, 2007. Print. 145.

2. U.S. Bureau of Labor Statistics. "Arts, Entertainment, and Recreation." *Occupational Outlook Handbook, 2010-11 Edition*. U.S. Bureau of Labor Statistics, 17 Dec. 2009. Web. 14 Aug. 2010.

3. Robert Reisner. *Bird: The Legend of Charlie Parker*. New York: Da Capo Press, 1962. Print. 27

4. Peter Archer. *The Quotable Intellectual*. Avon, MA: Adams Media, 2010. Print. 20.

## CHAPTER 2. WHAT IS A PROFESSIONAL MUSICIAN?

1. U.S. Bureau of Labor Statistics. "Musician, Singers, and Related Workers." *Occupational Outlook Handbook, 2010-11 Edition*. U.S. Bureau of Labor Statistics, 17 Dec. 2009. Web. 14 Aug. 2010.

2. Ibid.

3. Tim Ost. Message to the author. 25 June 2010. E-mail.

## CHAPTER 3. WOULD YOU MAKE A GOOD PROFESSIONAL MUSICIAN?

1. "What Is Suzuki? The Legacy of Shinichi Suzuki." *Atlanta Suzuki Institute*. Atlanta Suzuki Institute, 2002-2010. Web. 14 Aug. 2010.

2. "Facts and Stats." *Berklee*. Berklee College of Music, 2009-2010. Web. 14 Aug. 2010.

## CHAPTER 4. WHAT IS A CONDUCTOR?

1. "Arthur Fiedler: Boston Pops Conductor." *Evening at Pops*. PBS, 2004. Web. 22 Sept. 2010.

2. "Arthur Fiedler, 84, Conductor of Boston Pops 50 Years, Dies." *New York Times*. New York Times, 11 July 1979. Web. 22 Sept. 2010.

3. "Arthur Fiedler: Boston Pops Conductor." *Evening at Pops*. PBS, 2004. Web. 22 Sept. 2010.

4. U.S. Bureau of Labor Statistics. "Musician, Singers, and Related Workers." *Occupational Outlook Handbook, 2010-11 Edition*. U.S. Bureau of Labor Statistics, 17 Dec. 2009. Web. 14 Aug. 2010.

5. Ibid.

6. Geoff Edgers. "Levine is top-paid conductor in US." *Boston.com*. Boston Globe, 25 July 2006. Web. 14 Aug. 2010.

7. David Aines. Message to the author. 28 June 2010. E-mail.

8. Ibid.

9. Ibid.

10. Anita Mercier. "Pioneers of the Podium." *Julliard Journal*. Julliard School of Music, Mar. 2005. Web. 14 Aug. 2010.

11. Ibid.

## CHAPTER 5. WOULD YOU MAKE A GOOD CONDUCTOR?

1. Fred Parrett. "History of Jazz and Big Band Music." *Big Band*. University of Greenwich, Dec. 2006. Web. 22 Sept. 2010.

# SOURCE NOTES CONTINUED

## CHAPTER 6. WHAT IS AN ACTOR?

1. U.S. Bureau of Labor Statistics. "Actor, Producers, and Directors." *Occupational Outlook Handbook, 2010-11 Edition.* U.S. Bureau of Labor Statistics, 17 Dec. 2009. Web. 14 Aug. 2010.

2. Ibid.

3. Ken Sheldon. Message to the author. 11 July 2010. E-mail.

4. Ibid.

5. Mark Westbrook. "A Few More Quotes on Acting." *The Acting Blog.* The Acting Blog, 31 May 2009. Web. 14 Aug. 2010.

## CHAPTER 7. WOULD YOU MAKE A GOOD ACTOR?

1. Lance Carter. "Jenna Fischer's Advice to Actors." *Daily Actor.* Daily Actor, 24 Mar. 2009. Web. 14 Aug. 2010.

2. Philip Seymour Hoffman. "Acting Quotations." *The Jason Bennett Actor's Workshop.* JBActors.com, n.d. Web. 14 Aug. 2010.

3. "SAG Young Performers FAQS: Can I Earn a Living as an Actor?" *Sag Young Performers.* Screen Actors Guild, n.d. Web. 14 Aug. 2010.

## CHAPTER 8. WHAT IS A DIRECTOR?

1. "Show Business: I Dream for a Living." *Time.* Time, Inc., 15 July 1985. Web. 6 Sept. 2010.

2. U.S. Bureau of Labor Statistics. "Actor, Producers, and Directors." *Occupational Outlook Handbook, 2010-11 Edition.* U.S. Bureau of Labor Statistics, 17 Dec. 2009. Web. 14 Aug. 2010.

3. Peter Newcomb. "Hollywood's Top 40." *Vanity Fair.* Vanity Fair, Mar. 2010. Web. 22 Sept. 2010.

4. U.S. Bureau of Labor Statistics. "Actor, Producers, and Directors." *Occupational Outlook Handbook, 2010-11 Edition.* U.S. Bureau of Labor Statistics, 17 Dec. 2009. Web. 14 Aug. 2010.

5. Keith Stevens. Message to the author. 21 July 2010. E-mail.

6. Ibid.

7. Ibid.

8. Ibid

9. Colleen Simeral. "Shyamalan, Manoji Nelliyattu (M. Night)." *Pennsylvania Center for the Book*. Pennsylvania State University, 2005. Web. 22 Sept. 2010.

## CHAPTER 9. WOULD YOU MAKE A GOOD DIRECTOR?

1. Joe Neumaier. "Oscars 2010: Kathryn Bigelow's 'Hurt Locker' wins Best Director, toppling James Cameron's 'Avatar.' *NYDailyNews.com*. Daily News, 7 Mar. 2010. Web. 22 Sept. 2010.

2. Peter M. Gareffa. *Newsmakers*. 1991. Print.

# INDEX

## ABOUT THE AUTHOR

Marcia Amidon Lusted has written more than 40 books for young people. She is also an assistant editor for Cobblestone Publishing and a writing instructor, as well as a working musician. She lives in New Hampshire.

## PHOTO CREDITS